IMAGES
of America

OLD TUCSON
STUDIOS

D1613851

IMAGES
of America

OLD TUCSON
STUDIOS

Paul J. Lawton

Arizona Historical Foundation

ARCADIA
PUBLISHING

Published by Arcadia Publishing
Charleston, South Carolina

Printed in the United States of America

Library of Congress Catalog Card Number: 2007941880

For all general information contact Arcadia Publishing at:
Telephone 843-853-2070
Fax 843-853-0044
E-mail sales@arcadiapublishing.com
For customer service and orders:
Toll-Free 1-888-313-2665

Visit us on the Internet at www.arcadiapublishing.com

*This book is dedicated to the cast and crewmen of all Western films
whose hard work has shaped our view of what the "Old West"
was really like and to all those kids at heart who still believe
that the good guys wear white hats.*

CONTENTS

ACKNOWLEDGMENTS

In 2004, while cleaning out an old building to expand the technical department at Old Tucson Studios, I ran across several boxes containing old film records and photographs. I was able to salvage, scan, and file what were mostly negatives and proof sheets of the original pictures that were believed to have been lost in the fire of 1995. It was this discovery of more than 1,500 photographs that inspired me to want to share them with fans of Western films everywhere.

I would like to thank Pete Manglesdorf, the chief executive officer of Old Tucson Company, for his encouragement and support in the collection and preservation of these photographs. I would also like to thank Bob Shelton for his patience in answering the many questions I have thrown at him about the studios and people he has known over the years. Without Shelton, Old Tucson Studios would have never become the home to hundreds of films and television shows.

To my buddy Marty Freise, who knows more about Western films than anyone I have ever met, thanks for proofreading my captions and correcting all my "missteaks." To Karen Morrow, thank you for sharing your photographs with me and giving me permission to use them in this work. A big thanks goes to Jared Jackson, my editor; Scott Davis in San Francisco for walking me through "pixelation"; and the staff of Arcadia Publishing, who decided to break from the idea that a town must be lived in to be a real place.

Lastly, thanks go to my wife, Karen, who just smiled and nodded all those times I bounced ideas around and for being my best friend for the past 35 years.

Unless otherwise acknowledged, all images are courtesy of the Old Tucson Studios.

INTRODUCTION

Films have been a part of Tucson's history and economy for almost 100 years. In the years since 1912, Southern Arizona has been the primary filming locality for more than 500 films and television shows. By the late 1980s, Tucson was surpassed only by Los Angeles and New York as a filming location. A major part of the economy of Tucson and Southern Arizona has been based on supplying and servicing film companies working in the area.

In March 1912, the Lubin Stock Company arrived in Tucson with a troupe of 20 actors and filmed six "one reelers," each lasting about 15 minutes. The first film made in Tucson, *Renunciation* (1910), was filmed at the San Xavier Mission. The film *The Sleeper* (1912) used about 400 people as extras who had to dress in their own costumes for the filming. Like other film companies, they were looking for a place to make films free from the Edison Film Company, which was trying to find and prosecute other filmmakers for patent infringement of the film camera. This was Southern Arizona's introduction to the film industry. It almost became the capital of the film industry, much as Hollywood is today, with its 365 days of sunshine, an essential element because of the crude lighting systems of the time. However, as soon as the summer heat set in, the company packed its gear and headed for Southern California.

The Lubin Stock Company added $6,000 to Tucson's economy, a small amount when compared to the $9.8 million spent by the year 1972 by the film industry. In the years after the Lubin Stock Company left for California in 1912, other film companies came to Tucson and made at least six additional films.

In 1939, Wesley Ruggles read the book *Arizona* by Clarence Budington Kelland and felt that the story would translate well into a film. Ruggles, director of the film *Cimarron*, pitched his idea to Columbia Studios to make a film based on the book and to film it in Tucson, Arizona, the original setting of the novel. On a scouting trip to Southern Arizona, Ruggles found a site about 10 miles from downtown of Tucson. The area lay west of the Tucson Mountains and had a background of dramatic mountains whose northeastern exposure would allow for ideal lighting. The most direct route to this site was over a winding dirt road that lead to the Pima County Preventorium, a tuberculosis sanitarium. This would prove to be a tough road over which all the film equipment had to be transported. Leasing a 320-acre parcel of land from Pima County, Columbia Pictures allocated $2.3 million for the production, which in 1939 dollars was considered expensive. Included in this budget were the plans to build an exact duplicate of 1860s Tucson, Arizona Territory. Utilizing an 1864 map of Tucson and hiring 300 laborers, 180 carpenters, and 120 adobe brick makers, Columbia was able to re-create Tucson in just 40 days. Filming, however, was postponed until the spring of 1940 because of the threat of war in Europe. To bring realism to the film, Columbia rounded up every single stray dog in Tucson, 500 head of cattle, and 150 oxen and employed 250 extras and crewmen. The cast and crew lived at the Santa Rita hotel in Tucson, and during their off days, they would hold variety shows and benefit baseball games. The film starred Jean Arthur and a young William Holden.

When the film premiered in Tucson in November 1940, a weeklong celebration was held, and Tucson's population grew by 10,000 people. As part of the celebration, Kate Smith performed in a concert, a Papago (now Tohono O'odham) village was built on Congress Street, and a Menudo (tripe soup) dinner was prepared for thousands. There was such a demand to see the film that it was shown in five theaters around town.

Upon the completion of the film, Columbia Studios packed up their equipment and returned to California, abandoning the set to the elements. With no money available for upkeep, Pima County allowed the property to deteriorate. In 1946, the Tucson Junior Chamber of Commerce took over the lease for $1 per year and began to improve the site by repairing buildings and installing underground utilities. The chamber members (Jaycees) used the property to raise funds, including subleasing it to film companies for $60 per day for filming, and in 1947, they began a fall fund-raiser called "Old Tucson Daze." This event included live entertainment, a quick-draw competition, food concessions, and souvenir stands. In lieu of an admission charge, a donation box was set up near the parking area. Prior to the Jaycees taking over the property, the only film to shoot at the site was one scene from *The Bells of St. Mary's* with Bing Crosby in 1945 when Rainbow Productions used the old mission as a backdrop. This scene was eventually cut from the final release. However, during the tenure of the Jaycees from 1946 until 1959 more than 20 films were made at Old Tucson, including *Winchester '73* with James Stewart, *The Last Outpost* with Ronald Reagan, and *The Last Roundup* with Gene Autry.

In 1959, a developer from Kansas City, Bob Shelton, ventured west in search of a place to build an "Old West" town and turn it into a tourist destination. His first choice was Santa Fe, New Mexico, but while visiting friends in Tucson, he was shown the Old Tucson film set and immediately spotted what he wanted. He took over the lease from the Jaycees and set about improving the site. Forming the Old Tucson Company, Shelton invested about $500,000 in the property, constructing new buildings, adding restrooms, and creating an amusement area that included a miniature train, a haunted mine walk-through, a 1909 carousel that had been in use on the Mall in Washington, D.C., and a miniature automobile ride featuring cars bought from an amusement park in Ohio. On January 30, 1960, Shelton opened the doors of Old Tucson Studios to the public. On opening day, approximately 15,000 people attended the ceremonies, which featured Dale Robertson shooting through a ribbon with his gun and driving a copper spike to complete the miniature railroad. During the first year of operation, the park netted a total profit of $10,503.

Shelton then set about to bring film companies to Old Tucson and began to court the producers in Hollywood. With the aid of his wife, Jane, whose family included the founders of the Lowe's Theatre chain and what would become Paramount Studios, they were able to attract production companies to use Old Tucson as a primary filming location. From 1960 to 1995, one hundred ninety-four films and television programs were filmed at Old Tucson or its auxiliary facility, Mescal.

To attract visitors to Old Tucson, Shelton built a new amusement area in 1976, which included an expanded miniature railroad and a new haunted mine ride. Called the Iron Door Mine, it was based on a legendary mine located in the Catalina Mountains just north of Tucson. Heavy advertising and many promotional activities increased the number of yearly visits by tourists until, by 1995, the number of visitors to Old Tucson topped 500,000 and was second only to the Grand Canyon as a tourist destination in Arizona.

In 1969, Cinema Center Films Production Company began pre-production for the film *Monte Walsh* at Old Tucson and needed a secondary location with a more northern plains look. Spending $200,000, the company built the town of Harmony in an area about 40 miles east of Tucson on the eastern flank of the Rincon Mountains just outside the town of Benson, Arizona. At the conclusion of this film, the property and buildings were sold to the Old Tucson Company and became Happy Valley until the formation of the Mescal Corporation, at which time it was renamed Mescal. It has been used ever since as an alterative to Old Tucson as a filming location, and many films have been shot at Mescal, including the film *Tombstone* in 1993. At the time of this writing, Mescal is still an active film set.

Old Tucson became a full production studio in 1967 when a large sound stage was built and a full line of electrical and lighting equipment and a Chapman camera boom were purchased. To disguise the soundstage on the outside, a set of false-front buildings was constructed. This was the start of Kansas Street, a set with a Victorian flavor that would become the main set for the *Little House on the Prairie* television series. In 1970, at an auction at Metro-Goldwyn-Mayer in California, the Old Tucson Company purchased the studio's entire stock of wardrobe, becoming the owner of the largest Western-style wardrobe department in the world.

In 1970, Paramount Studios purchased a vintage steam engine, the *Reno*. The engine, built in 1872, has been used in more than 60 films and television series. The engine would be subleased to various production companies and transported all over the western United States to be used in films. On one occasion, the engine was shipped to Switzerland for a train show. Along with the *Reno*, the Old Tucson Company also purchased more than 30 pieces of rolling stock at the auction. Keeping only a few of the train cars, the studio sold off the excess stock to a museum in California. Several hundred feet of rail was laid on the north side of the studio by volunteer labor from the Old Pueblo Chapter of the National Railway Historical Society while dressed in striped prison outfits. Southern Pacific Railroad donated all the track, ties, and spikes used to lay the rails.

Over the years, Old Tucson was expanded to meet the various needs of production companies, and existing buildings were modified to change the look of the sets. One example is the two-story hotel that stands on Front Street. Built as part of the original Arizona set, a second story was added for the film *The Last Outpost* with Ronald Reagan in 1950, and then the entire exterior was given stucco covering in 1986 for the *Three Amigos*. This venerable building is now the venue for several live stunt shows.

In April 1995, an arsonist started a fire on the north side of the studio that spread rapidly. It destroyed 40 percent of the buildings, including the soundstage, the old mission, Kansas Street (home of *Little House on the Prairie*), and the entire wardrobe department. The fire was able to spread quickly because of a lack of fire suppression systems and a brisk wind. The large water storage tank was drained quickly, and the nearest source of water was several miles south of the studios. With the help of large tanker trucks supplied by the Tucson International Airport Fire Department and the U.S. Air National Guard, water was shuttled to the park. The old wood structures burned hot enough to warp the rails of the train line and caused a firestorm. It was only by the heroic efforts of many firefighters from almost all the fire departments in the Tucson area that any buildings were saved. At the time of the fire, about 300 guests and employees were present at the park. Fortunately, only two people had to be treated for smoke inhalation, and the petting zoo was emptied of animals without any injuries. The lower end of town, containing the original buildings from 1940 and the Silverlake amusement area, was untouched by the fire. The case remains unsolved.

After two years of rebuilding, Old Tucson reopened to the public in January 1997. New buildings were constructed, the mission was rebuilt, and a large indoor venue, the Grand Palace Hotel and Saloon, was added. With an emphasis on live entertainment and stunt shows, the studio is slowly rebuilding its tourist count and is actively courting the film industry. Several films have been shot here since the reopening. It still remains a popular place for banquets, weddings, and rodeos.

If you listen hard on a still, dark night, you can hear voices yell "action" and see the shadows of some of Hollywood's biggest stars walking the boardwalks along Front Street. Old Tucson is not only a historical town but also a place that helped to form the legend of the Wild West that should have been.

One

BEGINNINGS

In 1917, Sherman Productions filmed *The Light of the Western Stars,* an adaptation of Zane Grey's novel of the same name. The film was shot at the La Osa Ranch near Sasabe, Arizona. In this production still, the film's star, Dustin Farnum, is seen kneeling second from the right. This was among the first films shot in the Tucson area.

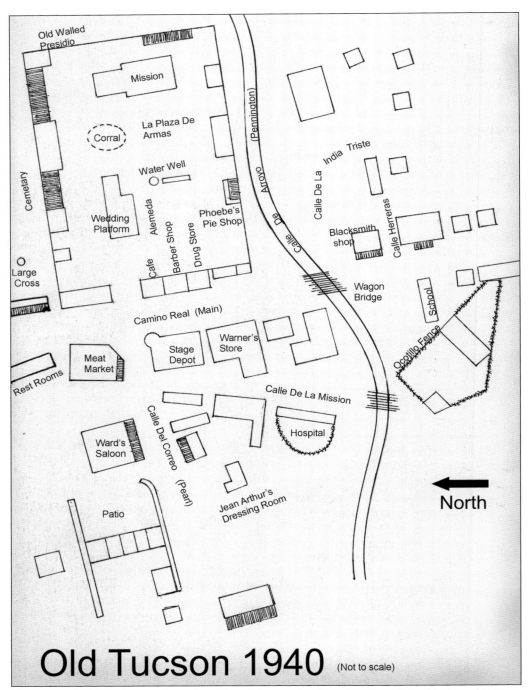

Old Tucson 1940 (Not to scale)

This map of Old Tucson was based on a hand-drawn sketch at the time of the filming of *Arizona* (1940). The design of the set was based on an 1860s map of Tucson. The street names reflect the names then in use. Camino Real became Main Street, and Calle de Arroyo became Pennington Street, their present names. Camino Real was also renamed Front Street for several films and is referred to as such throughout this book.

It took four months to build the film set for *Arizona* at a cost of $150,000, a large sum in 1940. Seen above are the Plaza De Armas and the interior area of the presidio. The prominent mountain in the background is Golden Gate Peak, which would become the signature mountain of Old Tucson and would appear in almost every film shot here. The photograph below is a view looking east along Calle de Arroyo from Camino Real and shows the reconstruction of the original wall built around the Tucson Presidio in 1776 by the Spanish.

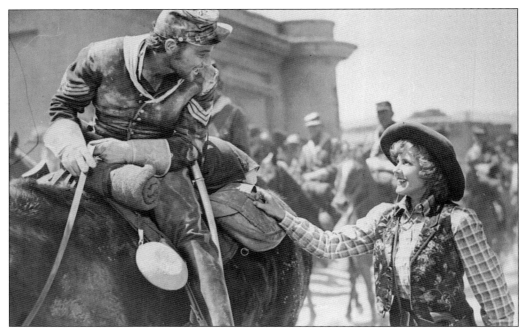

Seen here are William Holden and Jean Arthur. During the filming of *Arizona*, Holden was credited with saving the life of a man who was thrown from his horse during a stampede. Holden stood over the man, keeping him from being trampled. The scene included 100 Native Americans and 500 head of cattle.

Jean Arthur was, in reality, an accomplished horsewoman, and during the filming, she did all her own riding and stunts. Here Arthur is seen speaking with an unidentified person between shots on Camino Real. Note the early-style camera boom.

At right, Jean Arthur is holding several of the many stray dogs that were brought to Old Tucson as "streetmosphere" for the film. After filming was complete, she paid the license fee for each dog and adopted them out to local children, providing them with leashes and a month's supply of food.

Several of the buildings constructed for the set were made with complete interiors to facilitate filming. This is the interior of Ward's Saloon with Porter Hall standing on the right. This building remained intact until it was destroyed by fire in 1995. It became the location of the shooting gallery in the 1960s.

The original construction plan called for the buildings to be made from adobe bricks. Columbia Studios hired 120 masons to mix and pour the 350,000 bricks needed for the set design.

Among the hundreds of local people hired as extras were a group of Tohono O'odham Indians from the local reservation to give the town an appearance of authenticity. They are seen here making a Navajo rug and grinding corn.

World Premiere

NOVEMBER 15-16, 1940

Tucson, Arizona

Arizona premiered in Tucson in 1940 and was a weeklong celebration. Tucsonans reveled in the pageantry as Hollywood stars arrived to join the festivities. The film debuted in five theaters throughout town and was attended by an estimated 10,000 people who were feted to a Menudo dinner.

This still from *Arizona* looks southwest across the Mexican Plaza and shows the large number of extras used in the film. In the background on the right is the Stage Depot that was prominently featured in the 1986 movie *Three Amigos*. The building to its immediate left had a second story added to it for Ronald Reagan's 1950 film *The Last Outpost*. This building still exists on Front Street.

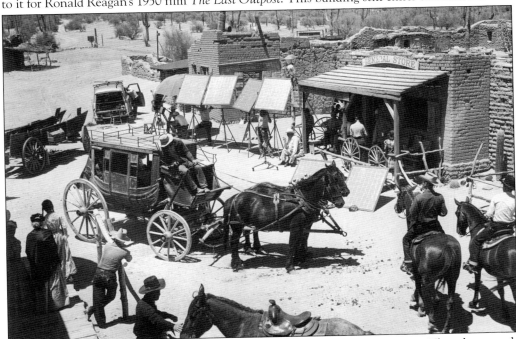

Also filmed in 1950 was James Stewart's only Old Tucson film, *Winchester '73*. This photograph of a stagecoach scene was shot at the south end of Front Street.

In 1946, the Tucson Junior Chamber of Commerce leased Old Tucson from Pima County for $1 per year. Using volunteer labor and donations, the chamber members (Jaycees) maintained the facility's upkeep, added a jail building, and installed underground utilities, including a sewage system. In this promotional shot, a fancy-dressed group of Jaycees poses for the photographer.

After taking over the lease from Columbia Studios in 1947, the Tucson Junior Chamber of Commerce used the facility to raise funds, charging film companies $60 per day to film. This is a photograph taken during the annual "Old Tucson Daze" fund-raiser, which was well attended, as seen in this c. 1955 photograph. The crowd is standing along Front Street with the mission in the background on the right. The building in the center received a second story and became the marshal's office in many films.

In a scene from *Strange Lady in Town* (1955), Pedro Gonzalez is escorting Greer Garson into Santa Fe. The scene was shot along Front Street, and behind them is the two-story jail, a prominent building on Front Street that establishes this location in films from 1955 to 1995.

Audie Murphy was the most decorated soldier in World War II and parlayed his fame into a successful film career. Here he is showing off his skill at training horses between takes of *The Guns of Fort Petticoat*, which was shot in 1957. The production crew in the background is setting up for another scene in front of the mission.

In this scene from *Gunfight at the O. K. Corral*, which was shot in 1957, the Earps (in the background) are prepared to shoot it out with the Clanton gang. In the opening shot of this scene, the Earps are seen walking down a Victorian street. It was actually part of the Paramount Film Ranch in California.

This scene shot along Front Street from *Buchanan Rides Alone* (1958) shows Randolph Scott standing over a fallen foe. The view looks south, and the buildings seen here are still standing at Old Tucson.

21

Clayton Moore (left) and Jay Silverheels made their only appearance at Old Tucson for the 1958 film *The Lone Ranger and the Lost City of Gold*. Much of the film was shot in Texas Canyon, 50 miles east of Tucson.

The building seen here is an original railroad station built by the Southern Pacific Railroad in 1900 in Amado, Arizona. It was moved to Old Tucson in 1959 when Southern Pacific closed the station. It acted as the first railroad station for the Old Tucson miniature railroad built in 1960. The building still exists and now contains a collection of railroad memorabilia, including a standard eight-day clock, an 1896 safe from the Gila Bend, Arizona, station, and a 1909 roll-top ticket case. The Native American figure seen sitting in front was "kidnapped" during the 1977 University of Arizona Rodeo and held captive until it was returned unharmed to a local radio station.

In the above production still taken during the filming of *Rio Bravo* in 1958, Walter Brennan (left) and John Wayne have taken refuge in ruined buildings during the climactic gunfight. These ruins are leftover walls from the Mexican village built for Arizona. This was the first of four films Wayne would shoot at Old Tucson. The photograph below shows a scene in which Wayne is about to exchange his prisoner for the character played by Dean Martin. Pictured from left to right are Ricky Nelson, Claude Akins, and John Wayne. The building behind them featured prominently in three of Wayne's films shot there and is referred as the McLintock Mercantile.

This aerial view of Old Tucson was taken in 1959 and looks north. The road in the lower left is Kinney Road; the dirt road along the top is Gates Pass Road, which was the primary route to Old Tucson from Tucson proper when the town was first built. The main north/south street in the center of the photograph is Front Street, with the mission being in the upper right part of town. Most of the buildings seen in this photograph were built in 1939. The barn structure in the center was built for *Rio Bravo* in 1958. Notice that the parking lot and admissions gate are on the west side of the town. In 1960, a parking lot and front gate were built in the immediate foreground.

Two

GROWTH AND CHANGE

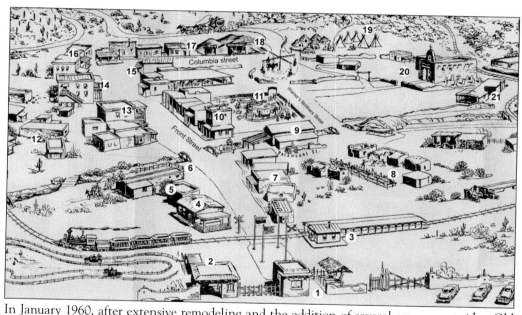

In January 1960, after extensive remodeling and the addition of several amusement rides, Old Tucson opened to the public. On this, the first tour map of Old Tucson, the key areas listed according to numerals on the map are as follows: (1) the front gate and ticket office, (2) the miniature car ride, (3) the train station for the miniature train ride, (4) the depot dining room, (5) public restrooms, (6) the stagecoach and burro ride, (7) the Mexican cantina, (8) the ghost town and gunfight venue; (9) the *Rio Bravo* barn, (10) the marshal's office, (11) the Bar-B-Que Corral and picnic area, (12) Ward's Saloon and Trading Post, (13) the two-story hotel, (14) the Golden Nugget Ice Cream Parlor, (15) the Red Dog Saloon, (16) the Valley National Bank and administration offices, (17) the mystery cave, (18) the Lost Dutchman Gold Mine, (19) the Apache Indian village, (20) the old mission, and (21) the Greer Garson House.

During the opening ceremony on January 29, 1960, more than 15,000 people attended the celebration. Old Tucson had 21 concessions, including a miniature car ride, a train ride, a stagecoach, the Lost Dutchman Mine, an Apache Indian village, snack bars, a Pan for Gold attraction, and a variety of gift shops. Here Bob Shelton, president of the Old Tucson Company, is seen addressing the crowd near the front gate. To his left, standing in the white hat, is Arthur Pack, the director of the Pima County Parks Department, preparing for his keynote address.

In 1965, the mission and Mexican plaza were extensively remodeled for the film *The Reward*. Bob Shelton is seen standing on the left, discussing the plans with art director George Chan. For the remodel, a cantina, a poolroom, a plaza, and a fountain were added, all made from adobe bricks imported from Mexico.

One of the first films shot at Old Tucson after it was officially opened to the public was *The Deadly Companions* in 1961, starring Maureen O'Hara and Brian Keith. In this photograph, a shot is being readied at the Mexican cantina from which Keith will make an exit through the door. This building still exists and is now Olsen's Mercantile.

During a break in the filming of *McLintock!* in 1962, John Wayne poses for a photograph in front of the Golden Nugget Saloon. In one scene, he will back Maureen O'Hara onto the balcony behind him where she will fall into a hay wagon. Wayne will then jump from the balcony into the same wagon.

In perhaps his funniest film, *McLintock!*, John Wayne plays a rancher who is trying to convince his wife (played by Maureen O'Hara) to move back home. In the scene pictured above, Wayne is chasing her through town and into the back of a barn structure built for this film. This building will play a prominent part in three of Wayne's films shot here. In the photograph at left, Wayne is chatting with O'Hara between takes during the filming.

In this scene from *Arizona Raiders* (1965), Audie Murphy (right) is standing with Ben Cooper in front of the mission set. Murphy made a total of three films at Old Tucson. Bob Shelton, president of the Old Tucson Company, played a prominent but unaccredited role as a gang member in the film.

John Wayne returned to Old Tucson in 1965 to film *El Dorado*, which also starred Robert Mitchum and James Caan. In this photograph, Wayne is throwing Caan a pistol while on horseback. This would be one of two films Caan would make at Old Tucson.

Seen here in one of the four films he shot at Old Tucson, Robert Taylor plays an old gunfighter out to right a wrong in the *Return of the Gunfighter.* The film began shooting in 1966.

In this candid photograph, Joanne Woodward takes a picture of her husband, Paul Newman, who is at Old Tucson filming *Hombre* (1967). The horse in the background seems unimpressed to be near such a famous couple.

The mission, built in 1939, was used in many films, changing looks as necessary, and has served as a mission, a saloon, a fort, and even a barn. In January 1965, after two years as a storeroom, it was consecrated as a church. The interior was decorated by Victor Boehnlein and A. B. Pinell from old lumber. Boehnlein hand carved profiles of monks and installed a cross made from a Cholla cactus above the alter. On January 31, 1965, Rev. Richard Rowley consecrated the mission as a church and religious services were begun. During the first service, music was provided by Reverend McCanon and his accordion. The mission is pictured here during the filming of *The Sacketts* with Tom Selleck seen standing on the right in the wagon.

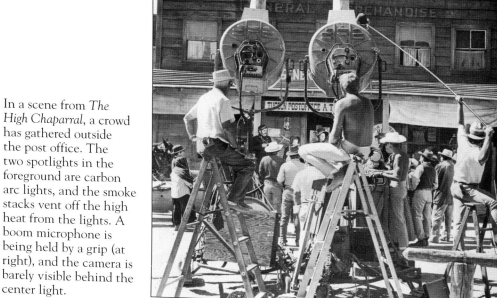

In a scene from *The High Chaparral*, a crowd has gathered outside the post office. The two spotlights in the foreground are carbon arc lights, and the smoke stacks vent off the high heat from the lights. A boom microphone is being held by a grip (at right), and the camera is barely visible behind the center light.

Filmed from 1966 through 1971, the popular television series *The High Chaparral* added a ranch set complete with a new barn. Seen in the photograph above are (from left to right) unidentified, Leif Erickson, Cameron Mitchell, and Mark Slade, preparing to repel an American Indian attack on the ranch. In the right behind them is the ranch house, which still exists. Notice the clapboard on the left, announcing the scene and take to be filmed. In the foreground of the photograph below, shot in front of the ranch house, are, from left to right, Erickson, Linda Cristal, and Henry Darrow.

Even with a pad, this stunt could hurt. In a scene from *Dundee and the Culhane*, shot in 1967, an unwelcome passenger is ejected from the stagecoach. Notice his spotter kneeling by the fall bag to help stabilize the fall.

During a break in the filming of *Dundee and the Culhane*, John Mills gets a visit from his daughter, Haley. Behind them is Southern Pacific Caboose No. 633. The caboose was donated to the Town of Benson by the Southern Pacific Railroad in 1960, after which the Junior Chamber of Commerce transferred title to the Old Pueblo Chapter of the National Railways Historical Society. The society, in turn, had the caboose transported to Old Tucson, where, with donated ties, tracks, and spikes from the Southern Pacific Railroad Company, a track was laid by volunteer "Gandy Dancers" (a railroad term for track repair crews) all dressed in striped prison costumes.

In July 1967, ground was broken for a $190,000 soundstage, which was designed to hold up to 3,000 people for social functions. This photograph shows the foundation and floor having just been poured. The building in the left rear was the Valley National Bank Building with the Old Tucson administrative offices on the second floor. The building to the right is the Golden Nugget Saloon. In the gap between the soundstage and the bank building, a Chinese alley was reconstructed for the frontier Chinese community.

To hide the soundstage from view and to add more filming locations, a set of Victorian false-front buildings were constructed. To give the set more versatility, the two-story buildings had removable fronts, allowing the look of the buildings to be easily changed. The buildings were designed by Hollywood set designer Richard Nelson.

Bob Shelton, president of Old Tucson Company, is seen standing in front of the newly completed, false-fronted buildings. The Victorian design was to offset the adobe, southwestern look of the rest of the studio. This area would become the foundation of Kansas Street, which would be used for many productions, including the main set for *Little House on the Prairie.*

Upon the completion of the soundstage, the Old Tucson Company purchased $50,000 worth of lighting and electrical equipment, including this Chapman camera boom. It is seen here during the production of an unknown film. The boom can still be seen outside the main gate of the park.

These photographs of the interior of the soundstage illustrate the size and floor space of the building. Shortly after completion of the stage, Paramount Pictures transferred the interior set of the television series *The High Chaparral* from Hollywood to Old Tucson. A set from this series is seen above during the filming of a dramatic building fire. The saloon set seen below was permanently constructed in a portion of the soundstage and appeared in more than 20 films. It was also used as the venue for live shows and a special effects show. The soundstage was completely lost in the 1995 fire.

Not all films shot at Old Tucson were Westerns. This scene from the *Miniskirt Mob* was shot in the Rattlesnake Pass area northwest of Tucson. The film, shot in 1968, utilized the Old Tucson soundstage.

Taking a break from shooting *A Time for Killing*, the cast relaxes while Glenn Ford reads the newspaper. Pictured from left to right are Max Baer, Kathryn Ford, Glenn Ford, Kenneth Toby, Todd Armstrong, George Harrison, and Harry Dean Stanton.

In *Heaven with a Gun*, shot in 1968, Glenn Ford plays a man of God whom townspeople believe is a gunfighter. In the photograph at left, Ford is seen hanging out his business sign. In a somewhat less formal moment, Ford (below) seems to be listening to something his horse is saying. He appeared in seven films shot at Old Tucson, more than any other major star except Jack Elam.

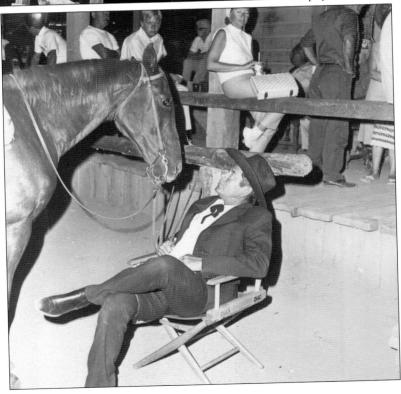

The long-running television series *Death Valley Days* filmed two episodes at Old Tucson in 1968. This exterior scene was filmed on the north end of Front Street and shows Robert Taylor (standing, center in street), the series narrator. The interior scene below from the "Pieces of a Puzzle" episode of *Death Valley Days* was the first production to use the new Old Tucson soundstage. Pictured are Robert Taylor, standing on the left and wearing the vest; Russell Johnson, seated at the table in the rear center; and Rudy Valee, seated on the far right.

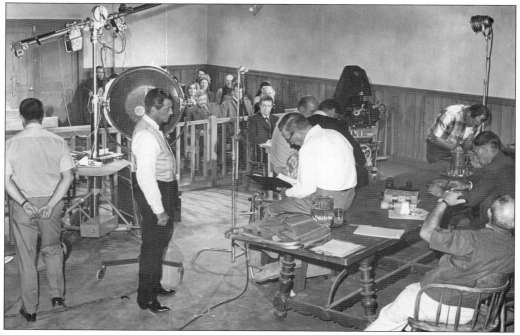

The above photograph shows Dale Robertson (left) and Bob Shelton. It was taken during the grand opening of Old Tucson. Robertson officially opened the park by shooting through a ribbon with his gun. He also inaugurated the miniature train ride by driving a copper spike into the rails.

In this scene from *Young Billy Young*, Robert Mitchum can be seen riding shotgun on the inbound stagecoach. Normally pulled by four horses, this stagecoach is being pulled by a camera truck. Behind the stage is the barn first seen in the film *Rio Bravo* and now known as the McLintock Mercantile.

Three

THE MOVIE FACTORY

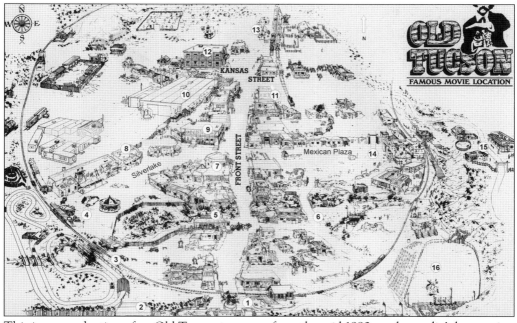

This is a reproduction of an Old Tucson tour map from the mid-1980s at the studio's largest size. The key buildings and attractions listed according to the numerals on the map are as follows: (1) the front gate and ticket office, (2) the wax museum, (3) the miniature car ride, (4) the railroad depot for the miniature railroad, (5) the O. K. Corral, (6) *McLintock!*'s barn, (7) the stage depot, (8) Ward's Saloon and Hole in the Wall shooting gallery, (9) the Golden Nugget Ice Cream Parlor, (10) the soundstage, (11) the Red Dog Saloon, (12) the *Joe Kidd* courthouse, (13) the main train station and the *Reno* engine, (14) the mission set and Mexican plaza, (15) *The High Chaparral* ranch set, and (16) the rodeo arena.

The popular and long-running television series *Bonanza* filmed eight episodes at Old Tucson in the early 1970s. In this episode (probably "Top Hand," 1971), Don Collier (left) and Lorne Greene are shown on horseback at the north end of Front Street.

In another episode of *Bonanza*, Michael Landon (left) confronts a deranged bad guy (Tom Skeritt) who has threatened Landon's life in the episode "The Hunter." Landon was closely associated with Old Tucson when he brought the television series *Little House on the Prairie* to town for its final two seasons. He also produced the television series *Father Murphy* and two episodes of *Highway to Heaven* at Old Tucson in the 1980s.

Before filming began for *Rio Lobo* in 1969, Old Tucson added a cantina and the "Phillip's Ranch" set just east of town and remodeled several buildings on Front Street. Also built at this time was the Rio Lobo River, which was supplied with water from a large concrete tank located upstream. In this photograph, John Wayne (left) and Jack Elam are seen exiting the cantina on their way to face down the bad guys. Notice the small fan in the foreground to give the appearance of blowing wind.

Victor French (center) is seen standing near the bridge over the Rio Lobo River. In the background is the barn built for the film *Rio Bravo* that has had an overhang added to change its appearance. Jack Elam will soon shoot a gunfighter out of the window located above this overhang.

In this photograph is a wind machine using a gasoline engine and an aircraft propeller. It was used in this scene from *Rio Lobo* to give the impression of a windy day. The building behind is the cantina built for the film.

In the film *Monte Walsh*, shot in 1970, Lee Marvin (right) plays an old-timey cowboy whose day is past, and he must face the modern world. Here he is seen talking with Jack Palance during a break in filming at Old Tucson. For this film, the production company spent $200,000 to build the town of Harmony about 35 miles east of Tucson, which became the site of Mescal, an auxiliary set belonging to Old Tucson that is still in use.

Beginning in about 1968, Old Tucson opened a contract postal station to serve the people living in the area and to allow tourists to mail postcards from the park. In order to simplify the process for the locals to send mail, Old Tucson moved an old baggage car to the area of the front gate, and with two entrances, tourists could enter from one end while local people could enter the other end without having to go into the park. This baggage car is still in existence and is now used for storage in a backstage area of the park.

Seen here riding the horse on the left is Brian Keith while shooting a scene from *Scandalous John*, a Disney film shot in 1971. Keith played an old rancher who is bringing his last cow to the town of Warbag. Sitting on the horse on the right is Alfonso Arau, Keith's hired hand in the film. This scene is taking place in front of the O. K. Corral on Front Street.

Thirty years after starring in the first Old Tucson film, *Arizona*, William Holden returned to the studio to film *Wild Rovers* in 1971. He is seen here in front of one the original 1939 buildings, along with Caitlyn Wyles.

In 1971, Johnny Cash brought his television variety show to Old Tucson to film an episode highlighting songs from the Old West. His guest stars included June Carter Cash, Roy Rogers, Dale Evans, Kirk Douglas, and Walter Brennan. In this photograph, Cash (standing center left) and Douglas (standing center right) are about to get caught in the middle of a bar fight.

This scene from the television pilot for *Bearcats!*, shot under the name of *Powderkeg* in 1970, features Rod Taylor (on the left in the car) and Dennis Cole (on the right in the car) as two adventures seeking their fortune in the early 20th century West. For this scene, a Stutz Bearcat automobile was driven through Old Tucson on a railroad track built especially for this film. The men on the left are holding reflectors to direct fill light into the scene. The mission is seen in the background.

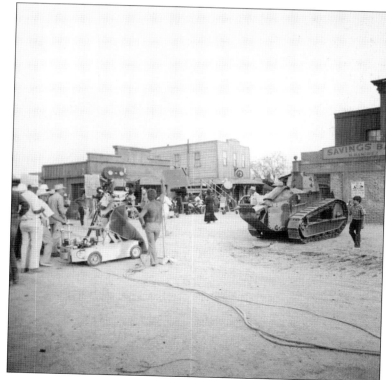

This scene from *Bearcats!* shows the first and only time that Old Tucson was attacked by a World War I tank. With the use of special effects, the tank fired several shells and destroyed one building. The series was canceled after 13 weeks.

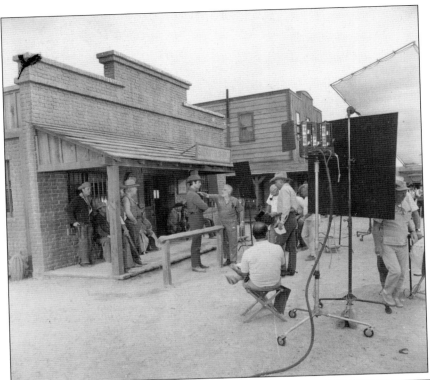

Clint Walker (facing right in the center of this photograph) is discussing the blocking for a scene in the film *Yuma*, shot in 1971. The scene is being shot in front of the sheriff's office on Front Street.

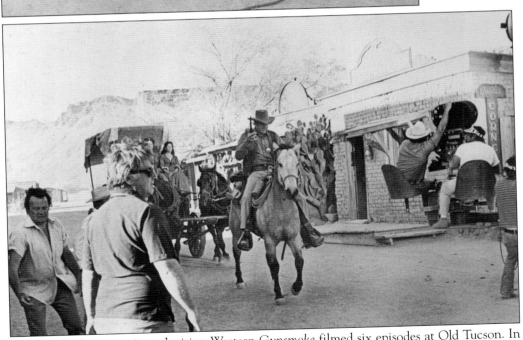

In 1972, the long-running television Western *Gunsmoke* filmed six episodes at Old Tucson. In this unidentified episode, James Arness, playing Marshal Dillon, leads a wagonload of women into town and down Front Street. Arness returned to Old Tucson in the early 1990s to film two made-for-television *Gunsmoke* films.

This photograph, taken from the balcony of the new *Joe Kidd* courthouse, looks northeast and shows the railroad depot built for this film in 1971. Nine hundred feet of new track and 200 feet of sidetrack were laid to the existing railroad for the film. This shot shows the beginning of a scene in which Clint Eastwood is going to crash the train into a building and begin the final gunfight. The real engineer, Gene Smith, is operating the train while sitting on the floor of the cab of the engine. The photograph below shows the result of the train crash, and the engine is seen sitting among the ruins of the building. The camera angle made it appear that the engine really crashed through a saloon.

The building pictured here is the courthouse built in 1971 for the Clint Eastwood film *Joe Kidd*. It was located along Kansas Street and was used in many films until it was destroyed in 1995. Look for it in the final scene from *Tombstone* where it portrays a theater in Denver, Colorado, outside of which Kurt Russell and Dana Delanie dance in the snow. The buildings in the background are the false fronts that hide the soundstage.

This photograph shows the set preparation for the final scene of the 1972 cult classic *Night of the Lepus*. It featured Stuart Whitman, Janet Leigh, and DeForest Kelley in a film about giant killer rabbits. About 30 live rabbits were used for the film, hence the need for miniature buildings.

A film about a Jack the Ripper–type character in the Old West, *A Knife for the Ladies* was shot in 1973. It features a Burns Detective Agency operative trying to track down the killer. Pictured here is Jack Elam, playing the town marshal, surrounded by light reflectors and a boom microphone. In the background is the train station located at the north end of town.

Filmed in 1974 as a movie of the week, *Pray for the Wildcats* utilized the Mexican plaza area of Old Tucson to portray a Mexican village. Pictured in this scene shot at *The High Chaparral* ranch set are, from left to right, William Shatner, Marjoe Gortner, and Andy Griffith. The ranch was decorated as a cantina for the film.

In a remake of the classic Zorro series, *The Mark of Zorro* was filmed in 1974 using the mission and Mexican plaza area, with additional scenes filmed at the San Xavier Mission south of Tucson. Ricardo Montalban is seen on the left leading a group of Mexican soldiers. In a break in the filming, Frank Langella, who played Zorro, is seen below in front of the mission set.

When the made-for-television movie *Backtrack* was filmed in 1974, it would be the sixth remake of this story. The first film was *The Three Godfathers*, shot in 1916, made again in 1919 as *Marked Men*, and filmed yet again as *Hell's Heroes* (1930). Finally, John Ford made two films, one in 1936 and the other in 1948 (both titled *The Three Godfathers*), with the 1948 film starring John Wayne. In the 1974 incarnation, starring Jack Palance, Jack Warden, and Keith Carradine, Old Tucson was used for production. In the photograph above, Jack Warden (left) chats with Old Tucson president Bob Shelton in a break between scenes. The *Reno* is seen below bringing a group of Confederate soldiers into town.

Marjoe Gortner (right) is seen in this picture chatting with crewmen during a lull in the filming of *The Gun and the Pulpit* in 1974. In this, his second film at Old Tucson, Gortner portrays a gunfighter who has taken on the identity of a preacher to hide from the law.

This photograph from *The Gun and the Pulpit* was taken during a scene filmed at the graveyard located just north of Old Tucson, which can be seen in the background. This cemetery still exists and contains several tombstones bearing amusing epitaphs.

This view shows a building on the north end of town along Front Street, which has had a second story added and portrays a church in the film *The Gun and the Pulpit*. It was not unusual for film companies to add to or modify existing buildings to meet the needs of the production.

In the film *Death Wish*, a movie about a New York man whose wife was murdered by a street gang, Charles Bronson travels west and visits an Old West theme park. While there, he sees a stunt show and gunfight that plants the idea of becoming a vigilante. Bronson, seen here on the right, standing on the porch of the Golden Nugget Ice Cream Parlor with Stuart Margolin, is preparing to watch the gunfight being performed by the stunt men of Old Tucson.

Kirk Douglas filmed *Posse* at Old Tucson in 1975; it was one of six movies he filmed there. In the photograph above, Douglas (left) is giving directions for the next scene to David Canary for a shot filmed on the soundstage. Below he is seen on the horse along with Bruce Dern, the main villain from the film. The engine *Reno* and several railroad cars were moved to a railroad siding near Florence, Arizona, for a shot featuring a train chase for this movie.

In a film shot in 1975 but taking place in the 1960s, *Katherine* had Sissy Spacek portraying a girl who becomes a political activist when faced with injustice in Central America. Here Spacek (on the right in the white dress and hat) is confronting Mexican authorities at the mission set of Old Tucson.

As any good horseman knows, camels and horses do not coexist well, and this scene from the film *Hawmps!* proves the point. The resulting chaos is clearly seen in this photograph taken of an overturned wagon on Front Street in 1975. Gino Conforti, playing camel handler Hi Jolly, leads a group of camels through town to a nearby cavalry post, filmed using the mission set. The mission was dressed up as a barn for this film, and a wall was built around the Mexican plaza area.

The 1975 ABC film of the week, *The Abduction of Saint Anne*, featured Robert Wagner and Kathleen Quinlan, seen here in a publicity photograph shot in front of the mission. Wagner returned in 1980 to film an episode of *Hart to Hart*.

The camels returned to Old Tucson in 1976 for the pilot episode of *The Quest* with Kurt Russell. In this scene, Russell (on the camel) is supposed to ride into a saloon and create havoc. The camel would not cooperate until the crew was changing film in the camera; then it decided to make its entry unexpectedly.

When the soundstage was constructed in 1967, the space created between the building and existing structures on Front Street was converted into a Chinese alley. It is seen here being prepared for a scene in the pilot episode of *The Quest* in 1976. Numerous Vietnamese refugees and Asian college students were hired to play Chinese people for the film.

In this cattle drive sequence from *The Quest*, the building in the center is the *McLintock!* barn. When built, it was designed so that it would appear as four different buildings if viewed from the four corners. This allowed the film company to save money on construction. In the far background is the wall built around the Mexican plaza for the film *Hawmps!*, which was shot just prior to the beginning of filming for *The Quest*.

In this scene for *The Last Hard Men*, Charlton Heston (right) and Michael Parks walk up Front Street with the old stage depot visible in the center background. Heston plays an old lawman who must rescue his daughter from an escaped convict.

In 1977, Michael Landon moved the production of *Little House on the Prairie* from California to Old Tucson. Kansas Street, running east to west along the north side of the studio, became Mankato, Minnesota. In this rarely seen angle, the north end of town is visible with the railroad depot on the left and the north end of Front Street in the center. Notice the engine *Reno* pulling a train into the station on the left.

In the above view of Kansas Street looking east is Mankato, Minnesota. Creative camera angles helped to mask the Tucson Mountains, seen in the background. The Ingalls family is just arriving in town and can be seen in the covered wagon in the far center. On the right are the buildings hiding the soundstage, and on the left is the *Joe Kidd* courthouse. In the close-up production photograph below, Michael Landon and Karen Grassle are pictured riding on the covered wagon in which they entered town.

Looking west on Kansas Street, Michael Landon is standing in the center in the white hat, waiting for the train to position itself for the next shot. The *Joe Kidd* courthouse is in the back center. Looking closely, an inside joke is apparent: the name on the *Reno* is Shelton, the president of the Old Tucson Company who was instrumental in getting *Little House on the Prairie* to move to the studio.

Perhaps discussing the next scene's blocking are (from left to right) Lindsay (or Sidney) Greenbush, Melissa Gilbert, Karen Grassle, and Michael Landon. Because of their young age, the twins Lindsay and Sidney Greenbush shared the role of Carrie Ingalls.

In 1976, Claude LaLouch filmed *Another Man, Another Chance* in both France and at Old Tucson. Starring Genevieve Bujold and James Caan, the first part of the film was shot in French, and the second half was shot in English. In this photograph, Caan is seated in a buckboard wagon discussing blocking in front of the train station. The film was released in France under the name *Une autre homme, une autre chance.*

In a sequel to the television series *Maverick*, James Garner returned to Old Tucson in 1977 to film *The New Maverick*. He is seen on the left as Bret Maverick along with Susan Blanchard and Charles Frank, who plays Garner's nephew, Ben Maverick. They are shown standing in front of the *Joe Kidd* courthouse.

Sandra Will (left) and Karen Valentine teamed up in 1978 to film *Go West, Young Girl*. They are pictured above in costume, relaxing between takes. As can be seen in the lower photograph, the mission and Mexican plaza area have been transformed into a prison. Notice that a portion of the wall on the right is not finished. Since this part of the wall will not be seen in the finished film, it is just used to support an interior wall. The crewman in the center is getting an exposure reading for the camera.

In the two-part adaptation of Louis L'Amour's third novel in his Sacketts series, Glenn Ford makes his ninth and last appearance in a film shot at Old Tucson. In this film, *The Sacketts*, the town of Mescal portrays the city of Santa Fe. The cast is seen here, standing on the porch of a building in Mescal. Pictured from left to right are Ben Johnson, Marcy Hanson, John Vernon, Ford, Tom Selleck, and Jeff Osterhage.

This photograph looks west toward the front gate and wax museum from the parking area. In 1978, Josephine Tussaud's company opened the Josephine Tussaud Old Tucson Filmland Wax Museum. There were 45 figures at a cost of $19,000 each representing various film sets from *Bonanza*, *Arizona*, and *McLintock!*

Shot in 1979, the failed pilot for *The Dooley Brothers* is the story of two brothers who have no skills but who head out west to do good deeds. In the scene above, the brothers decide to help with a jail escape. A special building was constructed to allow a portion to be pulled away using horsepower. In the center of the photograph is Robert Pierce, acting as if he is controlling the action, while on the right is a wrangler who is really controlling the horses. The effect worked well except that after the building came apart, it took about 100 feet to stop the team of horses and the jail cell. In the photograph below, the cast is pictured during a relaxed moment. Pictured from left to right are Shelly Long, Dub Taylor, and Robert Pierce.

Two sequels for the popular television series *The Wild Wild West* were shot at Old Tucson in 1979 and 1980. The two government agents, West and Gordon, have come out of retirement to again save the United States from some evil plot. In the shot above from *The Wild Wild West Revisited*, Robert Conrad (left) and Ross Martin are seen talking to a couple of unidentified actors. Pictured below is Jonathon Winters preparing for a scene in *More Wild Wild West* in 1980.

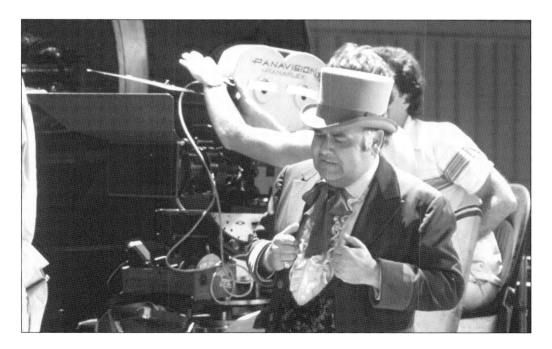

Three episodes of the sprawling made-for-television epic *How the West Was Won* were shot at Old Tucson in 1979. The above scene is from the episode "The Slavers," shot in front of the mission. The actors pictured from left to right are unidentified, Eduardo Ricard, Kim Cattrall, and Fernando Lamas. The photograph below from *How The West Was Won* is being filmed along Front Street in front of the Red Dog Saloon. Note the tracks on which the truck is resting to stabilize the camera.

Shown here in about 1987 is one of three stagecoaches built by Old Tucson master wagon maker Herb Holmes, who built many of the wagons used in the films shot at the studio. This coach is carrying tourists and is seen leaving *The High Chaparral* ranch set with the Tucson Mountains in the background.

Following the release of his hit song *The Gambler* in 1978, Kenny Rogers won a Grammy for Best Country Song, which went platinum and stayed on the top of the charts for 25 weeks. Shortly after the song's release, Rogers made a CBS made-for-television film of the same name. Rogers is seen here on horseback during the filming.

The television series *Hart to Hart* came to Old Tucson to film the episode "The Raid" in January 1980. The mission set was utilized in a scene is which a helicopter lands, delivering Robert Wagner and Stephanie Powers to a Mexican village. The scene would have been fine except that sand and dust kicked up by the aircraft's blades covered everyone with grit. The cast is seen here waving to fans as they arrive to film the scene. Pictured from left to right are Wagner, Lionel Stander, and Powers.

In 1986, CBS filmed *Dream West*, a sprawling television mini-series with Richard Chamberlain playing the part of Charles Fremont. In this shot, the mission and Mexican plaza area are being used as a battleground while the U.S. Army fights it out with the Mexican army for control of California.

A spin-off from the popular *Little House on the Prairie* series, *Father Murphy* was filmed primarily on Kansas Street in 1981. In the photograph above, Michael Landon (left) is setting up the blocking for Moses Gunn (center) and Merlin Olsen. Pictured below, Gunn (on the left in the wagon) is having a conversation with Olsen on the set on Kansas Street. The buildings behind them are false fronts hiding the soundstage.

When *Cannonball Run II* was filmed in 1983, the film was shot throughout the Greater Tucson, Arizona, area. In the shot above, the Mexican plaza has been turned into a casino, and other Old Tucson buildings can be seen in the background. In the close-up below, the actors shown from left to right are Dom DeLuise, Jamie Farr, Dean Martin, Burt Reynolds, and Sammy Davis Jr.

Seen here in front of the mission is Patty Duke, playing the part of a nun attempting to get a load of Apache children to Santa Fe, New Mexico, in the film *September Gun*, shot in 1983. She is speaking with Robert Preston, a gunfighter she has hired to escort them through the dangerous country.

Based on the semi-autobiographical story *I Married Wyatt Earp*, Josephine Marcus Earp recounts her years married to Wyatt Earp. In the film of the same name shot in 1983, Marie Osmond plays the part of Josie Earp. In this photograph taken in the soundstage are (from left to right) Ron Manning, Osmond, Bruce Boxleitner, and John Bennett Perry.

In one of its many incarnations, Old Tucson became Deadwood, South Dakota, in the 1983 film *Calamity Jane*. In this view looking east along Kansas Street, pine trees have been planted to give the town a more northern look. Notice the building on the right marked the No. 10 Saloon, the location of the murder of Wild Bill Hickock. Portraying the bigger-than-life character Calamity Jane, Jane Alexander is seen below taking a hat at gunpoint from an unidentified actor.

A modern cops-and-robbers film, *Flashpoint* (1984) starred Kris Kristofferson and Treat Williams as two Texas Border Patrol agents who stumble upon a jeep containing $800,000 and a skeleton. This discovery causes to them to become the targets of the government and a group of bad guys. In this scene filmed at the Phillip's ranch set just east of town, Kristofferson (left) and Williams speak with two crewmen and a deputy sheriff.

In the episode "Life of Judge Roy Bean," filmed in 1984, *Ripley's Believe It or Not!* used Old Tucson as the background for host Jack Palance, seen here standing on the porch of a building remodeled as the Jersey Lilly, which was Judge Bean's courtroom and saloon. The Jersey Lilly refers to Lilly Langtree, a famous 19th-century actress with whom Bean was infatuated.

Old Tucson underwent an extensive makeover in 1986 for the film *Three Amigos*, with a whole block of buildings on Front Street getting a coating of stucco to make them appear as a Mexican village. The buildings seen above will become a "Banco" and the "El Baracho Cantina." In one scene from the film, the three stars, Chevy Chase, Steve Martin, and Martin Short, will stand out in front of these buildings and watch an airplane fly overhead. Also to receive a stucco makeover, the mission received two new towers. The mission kept this facade until the fire of 1995 destroyed the area.

Adding to the existing buildings at Old Tucson, the producers of *Three Amigos* built a new set just east of town to be the location of El Guapo's headquarters. This building was complete inside and out and was used extensively in the film. Here it is seen with El Guapo's gang heading out to battle the three amigos. In 1988, it appeared in the film *Once Upon a Texas Train* and was then torn down because it did not meet county code ordinance. In the scene below, Steve Martin is getting ready to enter El Guapo's castle by swinging down on a rope from a watchtower. He crash-lands among El Guapo's gang and is taken prisoner.

In a remake of the 1939 John Ford film *Stagecoach*, CBS cast several of the most popular country and western singers of 1986. Shown in this publicity still for the film are, from left to right, Johnny Cash, Kris Kristofferson, John Schneider, and Waylon Jennings. Also in the film, but not shown, was Willie Nelson. The sign "Mankato" on the building to the right shows that the location is on Kansas Street, which was being used on the set for *Little House on the Prairie*.

In his fifth and final appearance in a production at Old Tucson, James Arness reprises the role of Thomas Duncan in the 1988 remake of *Red River*. In this photograph, Arness (on his knees) is seen with Bruce Boxleitner. The small building in the background is the schoolhouse from the television series *Little House on the Prairie*.

Portraying the famous gambler Alice Moffit, Elizabeth Taylor filmed *Poker Alice* at Old Tucson in 1987. She is pictured above in a scene shot in the soundstage, playing cards with a group of unidentified actors. During the filming, Taylor celebrated a birthday, and Bob Shelton, the president of the Old Tucson Company, whose wife, Jane, was a personal friend of Taylor's, threw a big party in her honor. Pictured below, Taylor and George Hamilton are serenaded by a mariachi band while shooting a scene inside a railroad passenger car.

Shortly after completing the film *Stagecoach*, Willie Nelson returned to Old Tucson to make *Once Upon a Texas Train* in 1988. He played the leader of an over-the-hill gang of train robbers. In the scene above, Nelson (left) is seen meeting Angie Dickinson, an old flame, having arrived on the stagecoach. Dickinson filmed a total of five films at Old Tucson. Pictured at left, Nelson has just been released from prison with the El Guapo castle from *Three Amigos* in the background.

ABC began filming the television series *The Young Riders* at Old Tucson in 1989, which ran for three years and included 68 episodes. In this publicity still from the series, the cast pictured from left to right are (first row) Greg Rainwater, Christopher Pettiet, Clare Wren, Yvonne Suhor, and Don Franklin; (second row) Ty Miller, Stephen Baldwin, Josh Brolin, and Anthony Zerbe. For many years after the filming was completed, the Young Riders fan club would hold annual reunions at Old Tucson. In the picture below, an explosion has just occurred as part of a scene shot on Kansas Street. The explosion was a little stronger than expected and only a quick response from the safety crew kept the building from burning down. Notice the pyrotechnician at the lower right just having set off the explosion with his "fire box."

Although Old Tucson is best know for the Western films shot there over the years, it was also a favorite place to film commercials and music videos. In this 1988 Duracell commercial, a rather small gunfighter has just arrived in town. At least 50 commercials used Old Tucson and Mescal as a background. More than 18 country and rock videos have also been filmed at these locations. In the photograph below is seen one of the "space horses" from the Kenny Rogers music video *Planet Texas*.

It was hard to tell exactly who the star was of *Grizzly Adams: The Legend Continues*, shot in 1989. The lead character was played by Gene Edwards, but in most scenes, it was Acquanetta who stole the show. They are seen here walking down Front Street, and although gentle, Acquanetta was given wide berth by both the crew and the extras.

Portraying the town of White Oaks, New Mexico, Old Tucson became a primary filming location for the 1990 sequel *Young Guns II*. In this scene, Emilio Estevez is seen leading a herd of cattle up Front Street just north of the front gate. For those interested in film mistakes, notice the audio speaker on the porch roof in the center.

Pictured above is the cast of *Young Guns II*, from left to right, Balthazar Getty, Christian Slater, Alan Rucker, William Peterson, Lou Diamond Phillips, Emilio Estevez, and Kiefer Sutherland. In the picture below, Estevez (left) and Sutherland are trying their skill at shooting at the Hole in the Wall shooting gallery. Fortunately, they used the guns provided from the shooting gallery and not the ones they have at their waists.

In this scene from *Young Guns II*, Billy the Kid and his gang have just ridden into the mission set. Pictured on horseback from left to right are Lou Diamond Phillips, William Peterson, Christian Slater, Emilio Estevez, Balthazar Getty, and Kiefer Sutherland (far right).

In 1984, View Master used Old Tucson as the background for a still shoot featuring characters from Sesame Street. This shoot would introduce Elmo to the world. On the porch welcoming Big Bird and his friends to town are J. T. Didio (left) and Robin Wayne.

In the 1992 off-beat, dark comedy *Stay Tuned*, starring John Ritter and Pam Dawber, Old Tucson became one of the places where the Devil tries to capture the souls of the lead characters. The photograph above shows Dawber (left) tied to a wagon full of dynamite across a railroad track, while a crewman takes a light reading. The railroad station pictured can still be seen at Old Tucson along the miniature railroad ride. In a relaxed moment, John Ritter (below) smiles at guests who have been watching the filming as he prepares for another shot.

This group of Mexican soldiers is marching into the area of the Mexican plaza in the 1993 film *Geronimo*. Note the crewmen on the roof in the center of the photograph. In the background Golden Gate Peak, Old Tucson's signature mountain, can be seen.

In a scene filmed at the main railroad station, a group of riders have just disembarked from the train and are heading into town in the film *Posse* in 1993. The day this was shot, rain and cold wind made filming rather miserable.

This scene shot in front of the mission shows the opening sequence from the film *Tombstone*, shot in 1993. In a moment, the cowboys will enter the scene and will gun down the wedding party. In the foreground can be seen the camera and sunlight reflectors.

The filming of *Tombstone* was split between Old Tucson and the Mescal facility. In this photograph, the Earps have just faced down the Clanton gang in a scene filmed along Kansas Street. The buildings at the left have false fronts that hide the soundstage.

As one of the last major films to shoot at Old Tucson prior to the 1995 fire, *Tombstone* is the final glimpse of the studio's north end at its height. In this photograph, the Earp brothers and their wives admire themselves in front of a reflective window at the main railway station. Pictured from left to right are Bill Paxton, Lisa Collins, Sam Elliott, Paula Malcomson, Kurt Russell, and Dana Wheeler-Nicholson.

Not everything in the films is what it appears. This photograph shows the *Joe Kidd* courthouse decorated as a theater in Denver, Colorado, for the final winter scene in *Tombstone* in which Kurt Russell and Dana Delaney appear to be dancing in the snow.

This candid photograph of Paul Hogan was taken as he prepared for a scene in the film *Lightning Jack* in 1994. Hogan's character has come to town to rob a bank and befriends a deaf mute, Cuba Gooding Jr., to whom Hogan tries to teach the art of bank robbing. This photograph was taken at the north end of town.

In 1970, Old Tucson purchased the entire wardrobe of Metro-Goldwyn-Mayer. All the non-Western costumes were sold off, and the Western costumes were integrated into Old Tucson's wardrobe department. In 1991, the entire *Little House on the Prairie* wardrobe was bought and added to Old Tucson's collection. The entire collection was destroyed in the 1995 fire. Shown here in 1994, the wardrobe mistresses are Kathy Murphy (left) and Rene Clothier.

Four

FIRE AND REBIRTH

This aerial photograph taken in about 1997 shows the present layout of Old Tucson. Much of the lower portion of the photograph contains buildings built in 1940 and not touched by the fire. The Silverlake area was also not damaged. Kansas Street was located in the upper part of the photograph just above the Grand Palace Hotel and Saloon. The railroad engine, the *Reno*, is off the top of the picture and is still on display. Key areas listed according to numerals on the map are as follows: (1) the front gate and ticket office, (2) the Old Tucson Museum, (3) the carousel, (4) the miniature car ride, (5) the station for the miniature railroad, (6) the O. K. Corral, (7) *McLintock!*'s barn, (8) the Arizona Theater, (9) the rodeo arena, (10) the town hall, (11) the two-story hotel, (12) the Iron Door Mine, (13) Big Jake's Restaurant, (14) the Grand Palace Hotel and Saloon, and (15) the mission.

In April 1995, a fire swept through Old Tucson Studios. It started at a location along Kansas Street. Because most of the buildings at Old Tucson were constructed as film sets, no fire suppression systems were installed, allowing the flames an unimpeded course. A stiff wind from the north quickly spread the fire through Kansas Street and south along Front Street and the mission area. The whole area of Kansas Street and the railroad station were completely destroyed. The photograph above shows the buildings along Front Street built in 1940 and used as the Mexican village in *Three Amigos*. The view below shows the west side of Front Street, illustrating the fickle nature of the fire. While the stage depot on the right was destroyed, the hotel building next to it was unscathed. The hotel building is still in existence, and it still has the stucco exterior that was applied for *Three Amigos*. (Both courtesy of Karen Morrow.)

In the photograph above are the remains of the Golden Nugget Ice Cream Parlor, while behind it to the left is the stage depot first seen in *Arizona*. The building in the background center was salvaged and is the present location of the shooting gallery. The fire did not damage the Silverlake area. Pictured below is all that remains of the soundstage and wardrobe department. At the time of the fire, only one large water tank was on the property, and all the water from it was used to cool off some large propane tanks near the fire. Therefore, the many fire units that responded to the blaze had to fill their tanks at hydrants located about five miles away. (Both courtesy of Karen Morrow.)

The heat of the fire was so extreme that the thick adobe brick walls of the mission were baked to the point that the building had to be taken down. The fire burnt away all the layers of construction added to the mission over the years so that in the picture above it appears the way it did when it was built in 1940. In 1996, construction began to rebuild Old Tucson. The photograph below shows the mission being rebuilt to its appearance just before the fire and in the same location it previously occupied. The foreground in the picture was the original location of the Mexican plaza. In the background on the right is Golden Gate Mountain. (Both courtesy of Karen Morrow.)

The new version of the town hall is seen in it the final stages of construction. When construction began, it was decided to widen Front Street at this point to create an open area called the town square, which now features a gazebo and is used for stunt shows. The inside of town hall has several interior sets to facilitate filming, including a courtroom, an assay office, a general store, and a bank teller station. (Courtesy of Karen Morrow.)

The previous inside live entertainment venue, the Red Dog Saloon, was destroyed in the 1995 fire, and a new venue was built in about the same area. The Grand Palace Hotel and Saloon was designed for both live shows and indoor filming. Located on the town square, it dominates this area of town. The interior features a large stage and a bar area decorated to the standards of the late 19th century. (Courtesy of Karen Morrow.)

Even though the Silverlake amusement area was not damaged by the fire, it was given a makeover to include a games area. Several of the skills games are shown here along with a popcorn wagon. (Courtesy of Karen Morrow.)

Moviemaking returned to Old Tucson in 2003 with the filming of *Ghost Rock*, starring Gary Busey. He is seen here confronting a group of townspeople in front of town hall. Many of the extras used in the film are Old Tucson employees and stuntmen. The author of this book is in a scene filmed at night at *The High Chaparral* ranch set while playing music around a campfire with Bill Camp. (Courtesy of the author's collection.)

In the more modern-era film *Cut Off* (filmed under the name *Taking Charge*), Old Tucson portrays an Old West theme park in which two fugitives try to hide from the law. In this scene from that film, Thomas Ian Nicholas is shown exiting the Grand Palace Hotel and Saloon to surrender to police. (Courtesy of the author's collection.)

In 2005, the History Channel used Old Tucson to film an episode of the television series *Wild West Tech* entitled "Gang Technology." The episode employed many of the Old Tucson stuntmen as gang leaders and members. In this photograph, Adrian "Ace" Martinez has just been rigged with a "bullet squib" for a scene in which he is to be shot. Pictured from left to right are Amos Carver, Martinez, and an unidentified pyrotechnician. (Courtesy of the author's collection.)

The mission was back in use for the film *Ghost Town*, filmed in 2005. In the scene above, the star of the film, Jason Wade, is just about to be shot off the top of the tower by another gunfighter whose hand and gun are visible at right. In the background on the right, pyrotechnician P. J. Lawton is seen with a paintball gun that is being used to create "bullet hits" on the tower. In the stunt below, Wade has just been shot and is setting up for a "roof roll," which will be completed by a stuntman. The two crewmen on the ground hold a blanket that will catch the gun and keep it from being harmed. (Both courtesy of the author's collection.)

Five

MESCAL

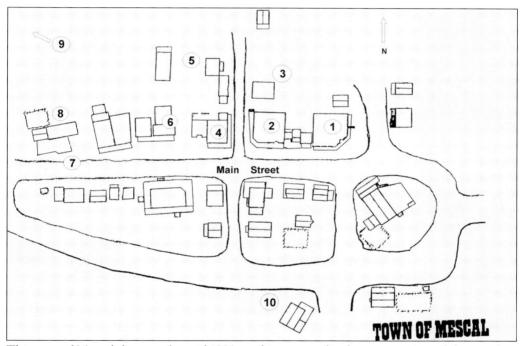

TOWN OF MESCAL

This map of Mescal dates to the mid-1990s and is a generalized representation of the set. Any study of Mescal is complicated by the changes various film companies made to the buildings to meet the needs of each film. The rooflines and porches have been changed, completely altering the appearance of each individual structure. The key areas listed according to numerals on the map are as follows: (1) the saloon built for the film *The Quick and the Dead*, (2) the Oriental saloon from *Tombstone*, (3) the general store built for *Monte Walsh*, (4) the Crystal Palace Saloon used in *Tombstone* and *The Outlaw Josey Wales*, (5) the shoot-out location in *Tombstone* (behind the O. K. Corral), (6) Jersey Lilly and Judge Roy Bean's courthouse and saloon, (7) the site of the Birdcage Theater in *Tombstone*, (8) the building used in the jailbreak scene in *Tom Horn*, (9) the fort built for *Buffalo Soldiers*, and (10) Virgil Earp's house used in *Tombstone*.

In 1969, construction began on the town of Harmony, located about 35 miles southeast of Tucson in Mescal Canyon, for the film *Monte Walsh*. At a cost of $200,000 and originally dubbed Happy Valley, this set became a popular auxiliary filming site for Old Tucson. Over the years, it would be such places as Cheyenne, Tombstone, Santa Fe, and a dozen other towns that needed a high plains look. During the filming of *Monte Walsh*, the actors and extras would dress at the Desert Inn Hotel in Tucson and then be bussed to the set for the day's filming.

Over the years, Old Tucson has built or rented various auxiliary buildings for use in films. This ranch set was built several miles east of Sonoita, Arizona, for the film *Monte Walsh* in 1970 at a cost of $50,000. When Barbara Streisand filmed *A Star Is Born* in 1976, she paid Old Tucson $10,000 to tear the buildings down so that she could build a smaller house for that film.

Old Tucson formally purchased the 2,400 acres making up the Happy Valley set from the Double X Ranch, forming the Mescal Corporation and renaming the town Mescal. Seen above is Main Street during the filming of *The Life and Times of Judge Roy Bean* in 1972. The oil derricks lining the street will be blown up and set on fire during the filming. Filmed later in the shooting schedule, Main Street is seen below as the location of a cemetery. Note that all the businesses seem to be owned by Judge Bean, although the truck visible in the center of the photograph is probably a little too new to be part of the film.

Paul Newman is seen above on horseback with a crewman in the foreground. Newman portrayed Judge Roy Bean in this highly fictionalized story about the famous "Law west of the Pecos" jurist. Relaxing between takes, Newman (below, seated in the center on the porch) chats with John Huston (right) and an unidentified crewman. Also in the photograph is a good view of a Chapman camera boom. Newman made a total of four films at Old Tucson.

This elaborate structure was built at Mescal for the film *The Hanged Man* (1974) and was to portray a foundry. In the scene below, Steve Forrest is trying to blow a hole in the foundry wall with a wagon full of dynamite and hay. He is being filmed by a camera truck and is about to jump from the wagon. The resulting explosion destroyed the center of the building. After filming, the entire set was torn down, and nothing of it now exists.

In this aerial photograph taken in about 1974, the area of Mescal is seen at the top of the picture, while on the right is the foundry built for *The Hanged Man*. As each film company used the town to film, it grew with the addition of more buildings. In 1979, a cavalry post was built in the area of the lower center of the photograph for the film *Buffalo Soldiers*. The town reached its largest size for the filming of *The Quick and the Dead*.

In this scene from *The Outlaw Josey Wales*, filmed at Mescal in 1975, a snake oil salesman is attempting to sell his wares to a crowd of townspeople. Clint Eastwood can barely be seen as he makes his way through the crowd at right. Also visible is a variety of film equipment, including a boom mic being held by a grip on the balcony. The film employed 200 extras and was in production for six weeks.

This view looking along the north side of Main Street shows the large hotel and saloon on the far right built for the film *The Quick and the Dead* in 1995. In the center is the two-story building remodeled as the Oriental saloon in *Tombstone*. By changing the rooflines and porches, the buildings completely change character, and identifying buildings through the years is difficult.

Gene Wilder is photographed looking a little out of place on horseback during his 1979 film *The Frisco Kid*. The film also featured Harrison Ford.

In the view above, rain has temporarily stopped the shooting of *Tombstone* in 1993. For this film, Mescal was transformed into the town of Tombstone, including the construction of a replica of the Bird Cage Theatre, which can be seen at the far center of the photograph. Notice the lighting equipment in the middle of Main Street that has been covered to protect the lamps from the rain. Below, a shot is being set up in front of the marshal's office. There are two fill lights dangling from the camera boom, and the street is still wet from the rain that plagued the film.

This contemporary photograph show the remains of the cavalry post built for *Buffalo Soldiers* in 1978, starring John Beck and Stan Shaw. Most buildings were not maintained between films but could quickly be upgraded and painted when needed.

In this rather dramatic scene from *Timemaster* in 1995, a fantasy story of a time traveler, a combination of propane, naphthalene, and explosives were used to create this explosion that has temporarily interrupted a hanging, stampeding the horses and the townspeople.

This contemporary photograph of the Devil's Plate Saloon, built for *The Quick and the Dead*, was taken during the filming of *Al's Beef* in 2007. This building served as the headquarters for Gene Hackman and his gang. The reflectors seen in the street are for redirecting sunlight into the building to light the interior for filming. The interior view below of the Devil's Plate Saloon shows the bar area in which Gene Hackman convinces Russell Crowe to participate in a shooting contest. Many of the buildings at Mescal had completed interiors to allow the filming of inside scenes. (Both courtesy of the author's collection.)

Six

THE *RENO*

The Virginia Truckee Engine No. 11, christened the *Reno*, rolled out of the Baldwin Locomotive Works in 1872 and was sold to the Virginia Truckee Railroad. It was sent to Nevada where it operated between Reno, Carson City, and Virginia City. The engine, a classic 4-4-0 steam engine, sports a balloon stack in this photograph, marking it as a wood burner. Here the *Reno* is seen at the railroad station in Virginia City in 1878.

In 1938, Paramount Studios obtained the option to buy or lease the *Reno* for $500. Its first credited film was *Union Pacific* (1939), in which it played the part of the Jupiter, seen here in the re-creation of the driving of the golden spike to finish the cross-country railway.

Metro-Goldwyn-Mayer acquired the *Reno* from Paramount Studios in 1945, and it is seen here parked in Sparks, Nevada, sporting a straight smokestack, having been converted to burn coal. In its more than 60 films, it changed its look by exchanging the stack, front light, colors, and cowcatchers as the needs of each film dictated.

Shown pulling into the J. W. Eaves Film Ranch in New Mexico, the *Reno* is seen in the film *The Cheyenne Social Club*, the last movie it made before being moved to Tucson under the ownership of the Old Tucson Company in 1970.

After its purchase in 1970 by the Old Tucson Company, the *Reno* was moved to Tucson on two large flatbed trucks and parked on 500 feet of track laid for that purpose. This would not be its last move; it traveled around Arizona and New Mexico for various films. It was even sent to Switzerland for a train show.

On this trip away from Old Tucson, the *Reno* was moved to a rail line north of San Manuel, Arizona, for the film *The Last Hard Men* in 1975. It is seen here pulling a baggage car and an 1880 passenger car, both owned by the Old Tucson Company.

Standing by the engine is Gene Smith, the longtime engineer of the *Reno*. He drove steam engines for the Southern Pacific Railroad for 30 years and piloted short freight trains from Globe to Bowie, Arizona. In an agreement with the Apache tribe, members of the tribe could ride for free by flagging down the train. Smith came to Old Tucson in 1970 and drove the *Reno* in all the films made between that time and 1995.

At the same time that the Old Tucson Company bought the *Reno* in 1970, it also obtained several vintage rail cars, including a crane car, a blacksmith car, and the passenger coach pictured here. It was built in 1880 and once carried U.S. president Ulysses S. Grant to Virginia City, Nevada. Surviving the 1995 fire, it now sits neglected on a spur line in the Old Tucson back lot.

During the 1972 film *The Life and Times of Judge Roy Bean*, the *Reno* is shown under full steam as she pulls the hill near Mescal, Arizona. Again she is pulling a baggage car and a passenger car (not seen). In her many incarnations, the *Reno* was painted in the colors of almost all the major railroad lines west of the Mississippi.

In the April 1995 fire that destroyed 40 percent of Old Tucson, the train station and the *Reno* were burned completely. Written off as a total loss, the *Reno* would rise from the ashes to continue her career. In 1999, Will Smith leased the remains of the *Reno* and moved it to New Mexico for the filming of *The Wild Wild West*. He had the engine restored and then returned to Old Tucson, where she has appeared in at least four more films since that time. Below she is seen in 2006 at the same spot at which she burned. (Above courtesy of Karen Morrow; below courtesy of the author's collection.)

Seven

THAT'S ENTERTAINMENT

Waiting for the stage to pass, visitors wander the streets of Old Tucson, where, for more than 60 years, the Old West of the popular imagination was created on the big screen by some of Hollywood's greatest actors. Looking north along Front Street, imagine Jimmie Stewart, John Wayne, and so many other favorite screen idols who rode hard and fought the odds to shape our memory of Old West history.

As part of the opening ceremonies in January 1960, Dale Robertson drove a copper spike to complete the miniature train ride that was built to encircle Old Tucson. The first engine to run the rails was the *General*, purchased from the National Amusement Company in 1959 at a cost of $11,666. It is seen here during the filming of *Scandalous John* in 1971.

When the park opened to the public in 1960, one of the first rides to begin operation was a miniature car ride. The cars were purchased from a small amusement park in Ohio and became a favorite attraction to future drivers, like the two in this photograph.

Two potential miners are seen here panning for gold with the help of an old forty-niner at the Pan for Gold concession on Front Street. It would later be moved to the new Silverlake amusement area and still operates today.

A perennial favorite with visitors has been the stagecoach ride. Here, in about 1965, the stage is seen crossing the Rio Lobo River in the Silverlake area.

This 1909 carousel was originally built for an amusement park in Slippery Rock, Pennsylvania, and was used for years on the National Mall in front of the Smithsonian Institute in Washington, D.C., before being bought by the Old Tucson Company in 1976. It would later be replaced with the carousel now in use at the park.

In 1976, Old Tucson replaced the *General* engine after 12 years of service. Shown here is the *C. P. Huntington*. This engine is still in service on the park railroad. In the background is the miniature car ride using new three-quarter-sized Stutz Bearcats, built by the East Coast Amusements Company. The *General* was refurbished and is still used in a backup role.

Based on a legendary mine located in the Catalina Mountains north of Tucson, the Iron Door Mine ride was built in 1976 and became a major attraction in the new Silverlake amusement area. Originally equipped with mine cars, it would later be converted into a walk-through attraction.

The Hole in the Wall shooting gallery was opened in 1976 in the old Ward's Saloon building. Shooters could try their hand at hitting various targets, including a piano player. After the fire in 1995, which destroyed this building, the shooting gallery was moved to a surviving building across the street.

As part of the Jaycees annual "Old Tucson Daze," the park would be open to the public, offering gunfights, cancan dancers, and various food and gift concessions. In this photograph are some dancers performing for guests at a stage located in front of the mission in about 1955.

Live entertainment became a mainstay for tourists beginning in 1960. That year, the president of the Old Tucson Company, Bob Shelton, constructed a false-front stage in an arroyo just east of the town. He would hire guest stars for personal appearances and to perform here in skits. Among these were Chuck Connors and Robert Preston.

The early-1960s entertainment would also include gunfight vignettes and musical numbers featuring four lovely ladies high-kicking the cancan dance.

Also utilizing this outdoor venue over the years have been popular country western and rock bands such as the Heywoods, pictured performing. By the 1990s, a large stage was built on top of the rise seen behind the band. This venue, called the Rio Lobo Stage, was used for a long series of summer concerts and featured such singers and groups as Kenny Rogers, Trisha Yearwood, and the Charlie Daniels Band. This arroyo area is now the location of the rodeo arena.

The streets of Old Tucson could become crowded as guests jam the area for a performance of the Old Tucson stuntmen on Front Street. By the mid-1980s, Old Tucson was drawing half a million visitors a year, second only to the Grand Canyon as a tourist attraction. This photograph was taken in the late 1960s.

What Old West town would be complete without a gunfight and stunt show? Old Tucson has performed these gunfights at various venues over the years. In this photograph, Amos Carver is beating on James Mead while guests watch in the background.

In 1975, Old Tucson constructed a full-sized rodeo arena to host the annual University of Arizona Rodeo. The arena was also used by for the Pima Community College Rodeo and the Law Enforcement Rodeo Association's Tucson Rodeo. It is still in use today for corporate rodeos and a spring, Saturday night, rodeo series.

The Dr. W. W. Wheezer Medicine show has been performed live at Old Tucson since the early 1980s and is still a popular production about a snake oil salesman trying to peddle his wares to unsuspecting, gullible guests. This photograph from the 1986 shows Robin Wayne (left) and William Morton in front of the medicine wagon.

In the summer of 1973, the Arizona Civic Theatre performed in a 10-week run of *Diamond Studs*, a musical story of the life of Jesse James. Pictured from left to right are (on the main floor) Jim Griffith, Dave Luckow, Cindy Danno, Ed Davenport, Rena Cook, Phil Stover (as Jesse James), and Ron Doering while watching from the balcony are Chip Curry (left) and Gary Farrel.

In addition to the outside attractions, the Red Dog Saloon hosted a variety of musical shows. This is a photograph taken during a performance of the "Miss Jubilee Jones" show, featuring, from left to right, Kelley Bertenshaw, Blake De Mar, Glenda Young, and two unidentified dancers.

After the Red Dog Saloon was destroyed in the 1995 fire, a new, inside venue was constructed. The Grand Palace Hotel and Saloon was designed for both live musical shows and for filming. Seen here during a performance of the "Raise a Ruckus" musical show are, from left to right, Janet Roby, Sara Carver, Seonaid Barngrover, Nathan Delahay, and Matt Stareka. (Courtesy of the author's collection.)

This is the grizzly end of a botched bank robbery from the gunfight and stunt show, "The Great Tucson Bank Robbery," performed in the town square. Pictured from left to right are Nate Delahey, Aaron Arraza, and Sara Carver. (Courtesy of the author's collection.)

The mission set is still an active venue for live stunt shows. This 2003 photograph was taken during a performance of the comedy stunt show "The Three Amigos." Pictured are Sara Carver (left) and Jason Cabrera reacting to the exploding building. (Courtesy of the author's collection.)

Beginning in 1989, Old Tucson introduced "Nightfall," a special Halloween celebration, and in 1990, it became a permanent annual event. Performed during the month of October, the park is open at night as the town of Nightfall. The event centers on several special shows and scary walk-through attractions.

This production still shows the cast of the 2003 indoor Nightfall musical production. Pictured from left to right are (first row) Juoy Luzania, Josh Van Wienen, and Sara Carver; (second row) Josh Staffeld, Laura Wood, Michael Hawk, and Bill Camp. (Courtesy of the author's collection.)

The town of Nightfall is run by the evil Dr. Jebediah Hyde, a mad doctor who turned the town into a mental institution. The event, still being held each year, draws more than 50,000 visitors during October evenings. Seen here trying to control two inmates is Josh Coyan as Dr. Hyde; behind him are Mark Bruger and Lisa Meeder.

DISCOVER THOUSANDS OF LOCAL HISTORY BOOKS FEATURING MILLIONS OF VINTAGE IMAGES

Arcadia Publishing, the leading local history publisher in the United States, is committed to making history accessible and meaningful through publishing books that celebrate and preserve the heritage of America's people and places.

Find more books like this at
www.arcadiapublishing.com

Search for your hometown history, your old stomping grounds, and even your favorite sports team.